God's Gift

God's Gift

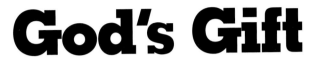

Over 100 Studs, Stallions, and Dreamboats from the 70s and 80s

Abrams Image
New York

Gift List

Foreword

YOU NEVER FORGET your first love. And I'm not talking about the pimply compatriots of your youth, or even that dangerous older boy who—shock, horror!—smoked cigarettes *on school grounds*. Instead, think back to the time when your favorite pin-ups ruled your world— when your bedroom was plastered floor to ceiling with technicolored talent; pencil cases and school books were smothered in stickers bearing your beloved's image; and nights were spent imagining yourself as Mrs. Michael J. Fox, or Mrs. Richard Gere, or Mrs. Sean Connery... (decisions, decisions). Ah, those were the days. Back then, we all had our very own perfect pseudo-boyfriends—heroes who would never let us down, pull our hair, or shriek, "Girls smell!" Those guys really had it all: fabulous physiques, come-to-bed eyes, macho charisma yet soulful sensitivity... and of course in our lovestruck imaginations they had eyes only for us. No wonder they stole our hearts. Forget, for the moment, the dodgy fashion sense and the questionable poses; remember instead the blissful hours of stargazing and daydreaming that these pin-ups afforded us.

Yes, for every girl (or guy) who has worshipped at the altar of Adonis, this is a chance to revisit those glorious years when a whole afternoon could be spent in devoted contemplation of a single, slightly dog-eared, Christian Slater poster. Taking a mouthwatering meander through the pin-ups of the past, *God's Gift* catalogues the cutest smiles, whitest teeth, and cheesiest poses ever to be caught on camera. Inside these pages, over one hundred hot hunks await your discerning eye, their good looks and bronzed bodies crying out to be ogled. If you have ever gazed wistfully at a pair of gleaming pecs, or yearned to trail your fingers over the corrugated contours of a washboard stomach, this is the book for you.

All the tools, the attributes, the accessories of male seductive charm are here, and in all their understated glory: the long, lithe limbs; the toned, tanned torso; the impossibly dense mane of hair (or, for the less hirsutely gifted, the carefully polished pate); the teasing, come-hither glance; the dazzling, predatory smile; the glitzy medallion; the tight, cheese-cutter jeans; the navel-skimming Hawaiian shirt; the saucy Stetson.... From the Brat Pack to the Bee Gees, David Cassidy to David Hasselhoff, Adam Ant to Duran Duran, *God's Gift* lays on a feast for all, with torsos to tempt every taste-bud. Do studmuffins from the seventies float your boat? Or was it the heartthrobs of the eighties that set your pulse racing and your temperature rising? Be it country-and-western cowboys, butch bikers, silver-screen sex bombs, or raunchy warblers that take your breath away, *God's Gift* delivers on every front (and, in the case of racing driver James Hunt, very nearly full frontal).

Of course, dreamy though these gentlemen are, we ladies are no longer the star-struck, (not so) bright young things we once were. We now have jobs, handbags, breasts, and all the other grown-up paraphernalia maturity brings. And—um, how shall I put this?—in some cases our tastes have moved on, too. While a fleet of dreamboats are still seaworthy, with snapshots showing them to be fully rigged and ready even after all these years, others aren't quite so, well, shipshape. Be it fashion fiascos, hairdo horrors, or a simple case of "What *were* they thinking?" *God's Gift* is not afraid to include the pics that some stars might prefer us *not* to revisit: early shots of modern-day marvels (eat your heart out, Brad Pitt); a potpourri of peculiar poses (and poseurs); cheesy chaps who really put the *fromage* into a photo shoot; and rock stars who are open for ridicule. Gaze and wonder why we (and they) ever thought they looked hot, hot, hot—while secretly thinking that there's just something about a mullet on a man . . .

Call it nostalgia, call it lechery, call it the ideal way to spend an afternoon—there's no doubting that *God's Gift* is utterly irresistible. Crowded with snaps of the guys who once made us weak at the knees, every page is an homage to the hunk, a celebration of the sex symbol, a tribute to testosterone that will keep you up all night. Relish the reunion with singers who made us swoon, actors who made us ache with longing, and sports stars who made us realize P.E. wasn't all bad. You can keep your groomed and polished Messrs. Timberlake, Beckham, and DiCaprio—the real deal's right here: before stylists and airbrushing; before celebs caught on to controlling their images; before most of today's stars were even born. Give us love handles, frizz, and outrageous costumes. Give us macho men, bodybuilders, and lovelorn-looking boys. Give us naked flesh, baby oil, and seriously bad hair days. Forget the man-made...here are the real men.

So switch your phone to automatic voice mail, don't answer the door, and put your out-of-office response on your e-mail. Turn all your attention to the tasty treats to follow. Prepare for a provocative experience that will make you giggle, sigh, smile, and reminisce. Let yourself once more fall under the spell of these hairy beefcakes, these seductive señores, these

Burt Reynolds outsmoldering his cigar, as usual.

Tom Cruise:
Position Impossible.

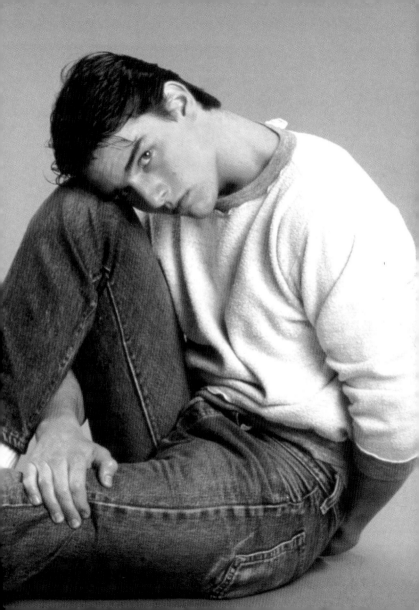

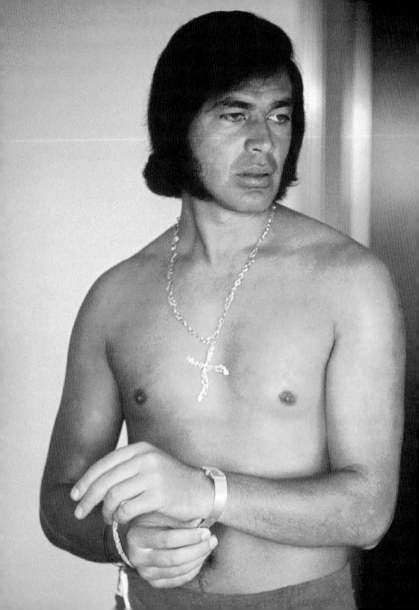

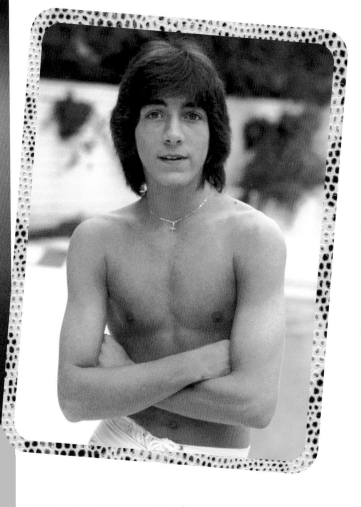

◀ ***Engelbert Humperdinck****:*
original King of Bling.

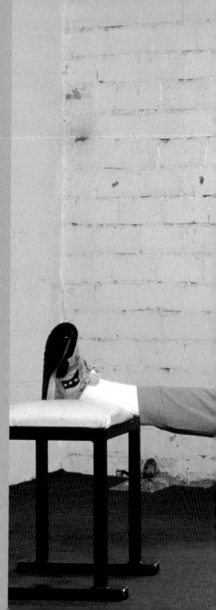

*Keep smiling, **Jean-Claude Van Damme**—perhaps no one will notice you've forgotten your weights.*

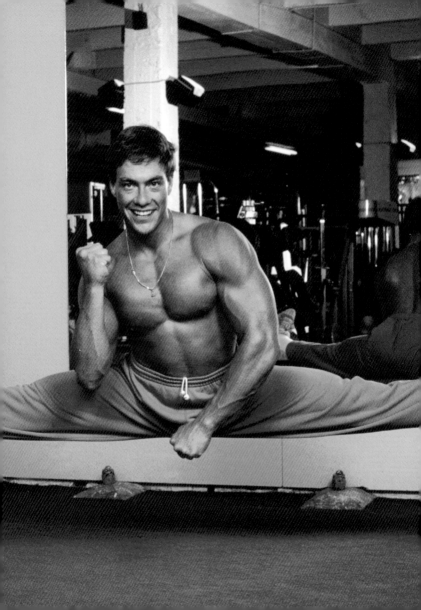

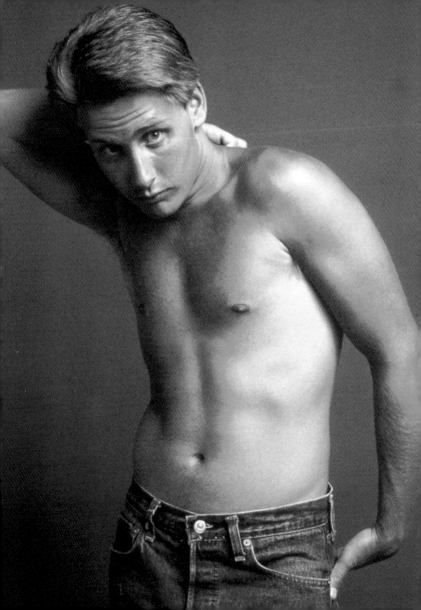

Sylvester Stallone: less Rambo, more Pretty in Pink.

◀ *Emilio Estevez* worries that his deodorant isn't working.

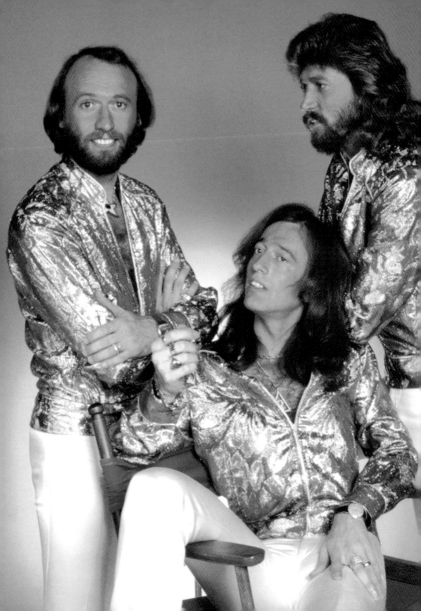

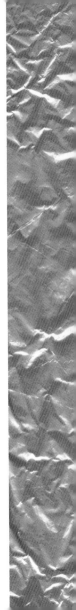

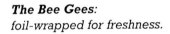

The Bee Gees:
foil-wrapped for freshness.

Europe provide the final countdown for mullets everywhere.

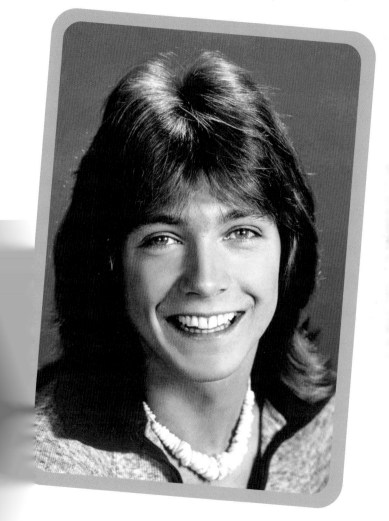

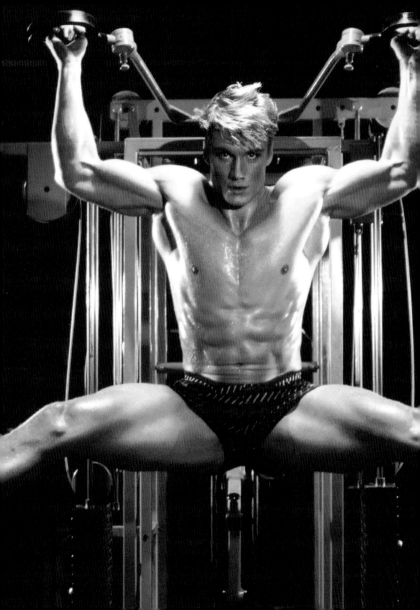

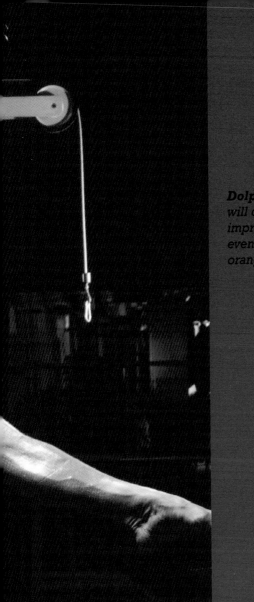

Dolph Lundgren will do anything to impress the ladies— even grow a pair of orange antlers.

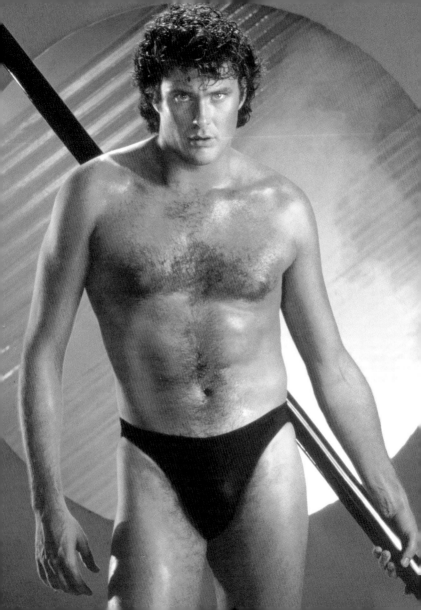

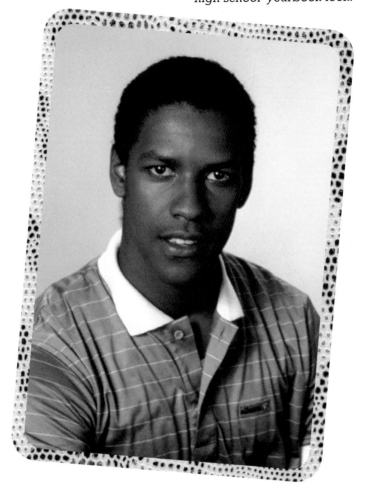

Denzel Washington works the high school–yearbook look.

◀ *David Hasselhoff*: small pants, big pole.

Corey Haim: *this lost boy's*
(trying to be) all man.

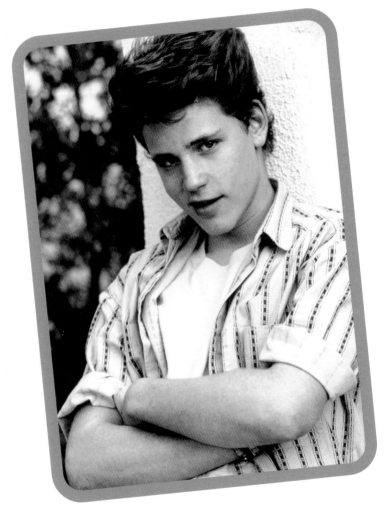

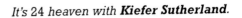

◀ **Paul Stanley** *from KISS dresses to the right.*

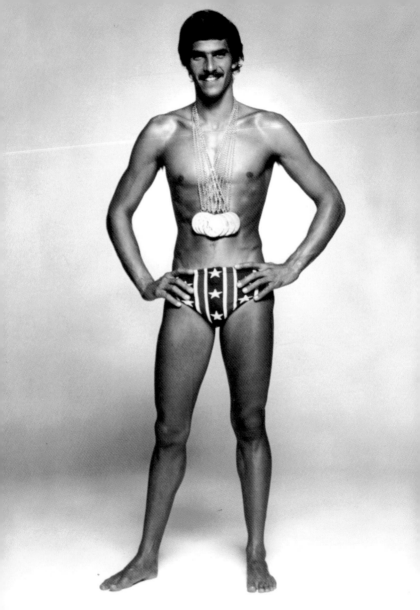

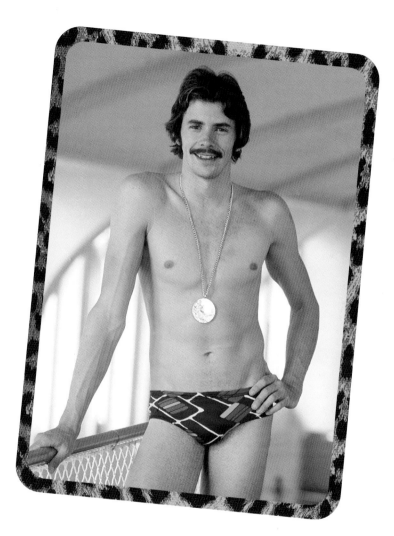

Mark Spitz (left) and **David Wilkie** proudly show off
the chocolate money Santa gave them.   23

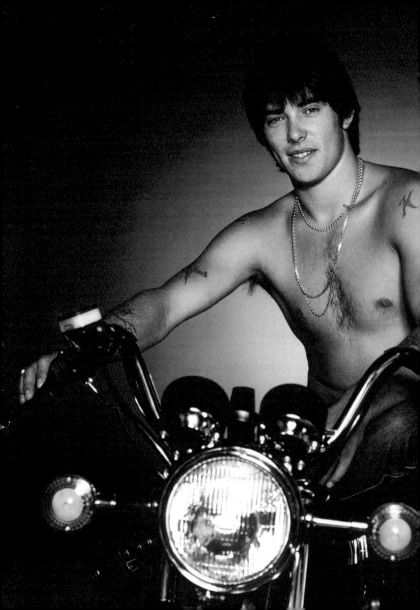

Eddie Kidd: famed
for the throbbing beast
between his legs.

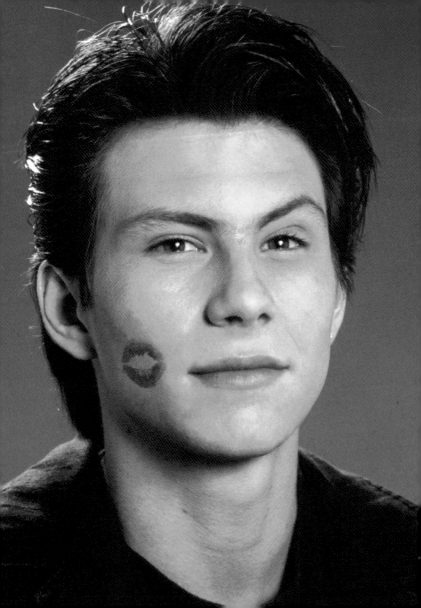

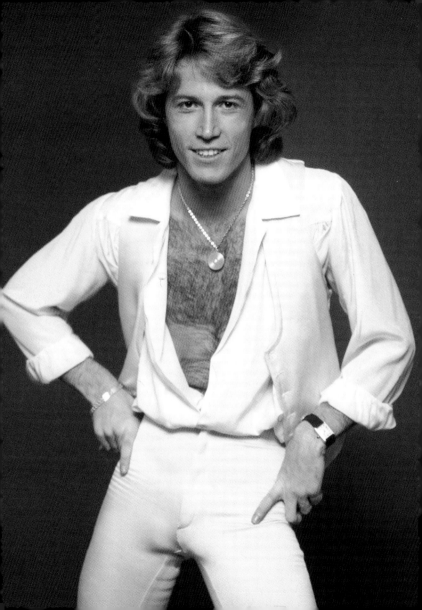

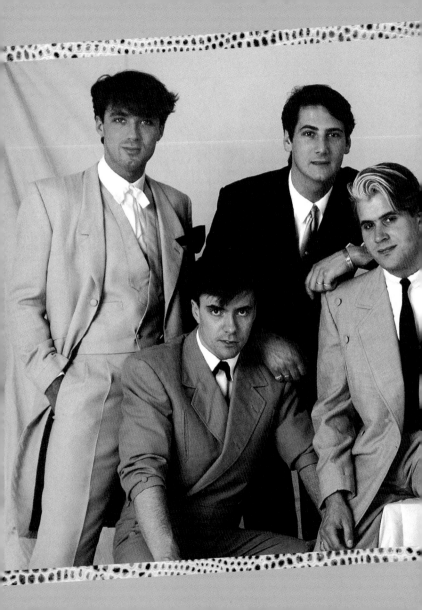

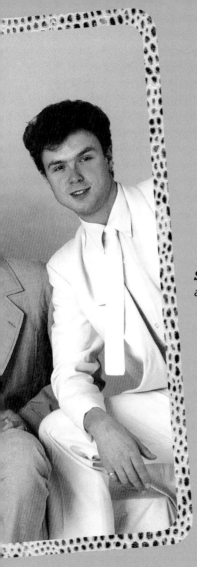

Spandau Ballet love
a good wedding.

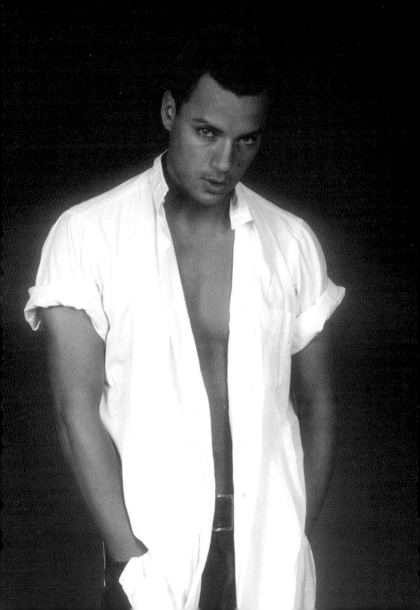

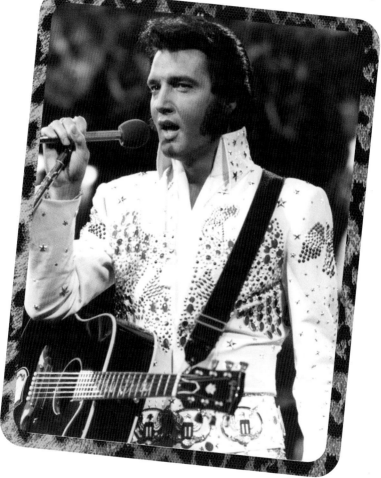

We won't let you be lonesome tonight, **Elvis Presley**.

◀ **Nick Kamen**—*sadly, just before he put the Levi's in for a wash.*

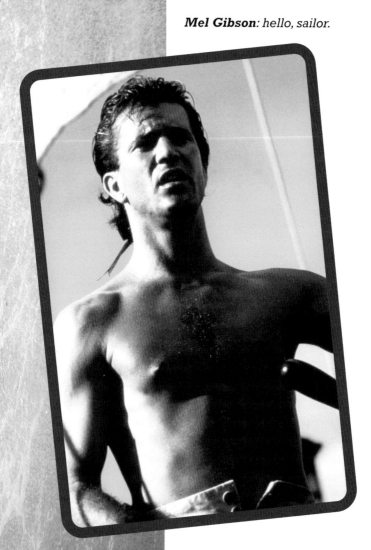

Mel Gibson: *hello, sailor.*

Eddie Murphy: ▶
(Beverly Hills) Cop *a load of this!*

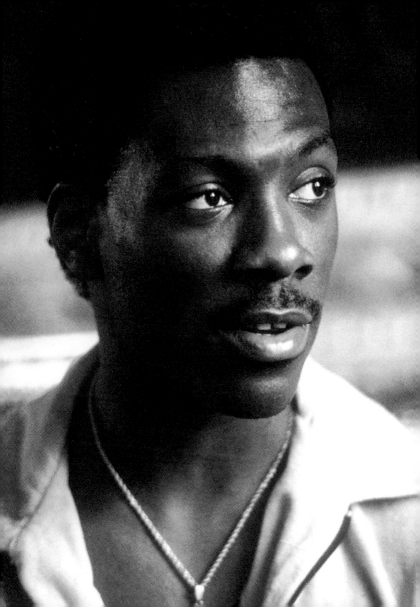

Andrew McCarthy:
pretty in pastel.

Starsky and Hutch: *crime capers in casual knitwear.*

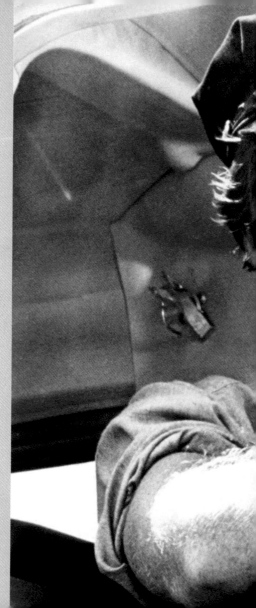

*One look from **Robert Redford** jams all the ladies' frequencies.*

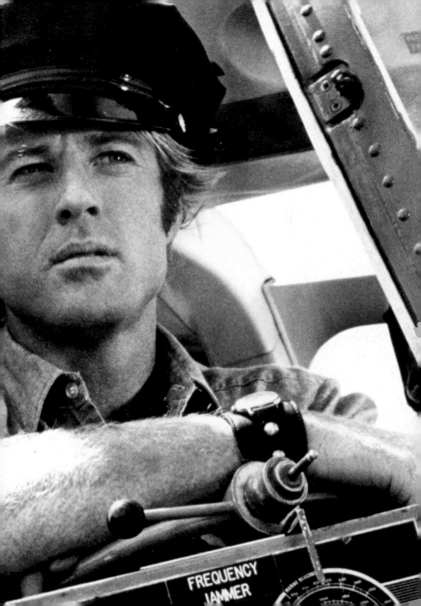

FREQUENCY
JAMMER

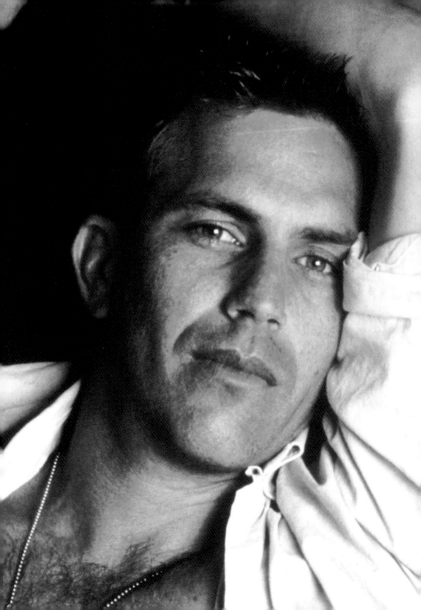

*Nobody puts (**Patrick**)*
Swayze *in the corner.*

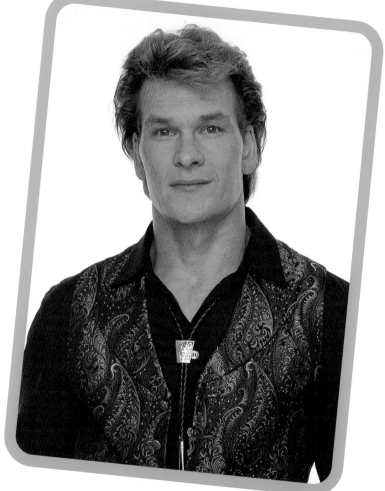

◀ ***Kevin Costner:*** *I will*
always love me.

Warren Beatty: so vain, he probably thinks this caption's about him.

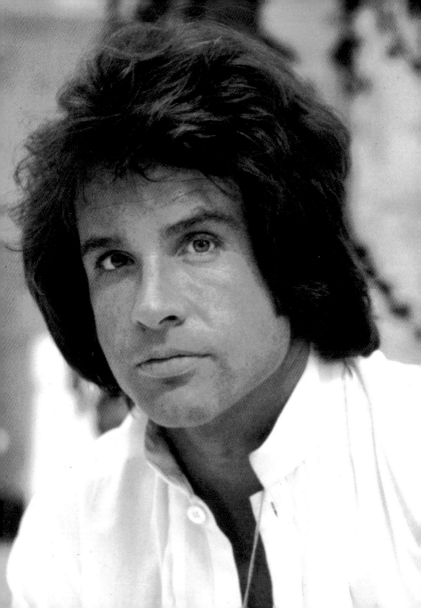

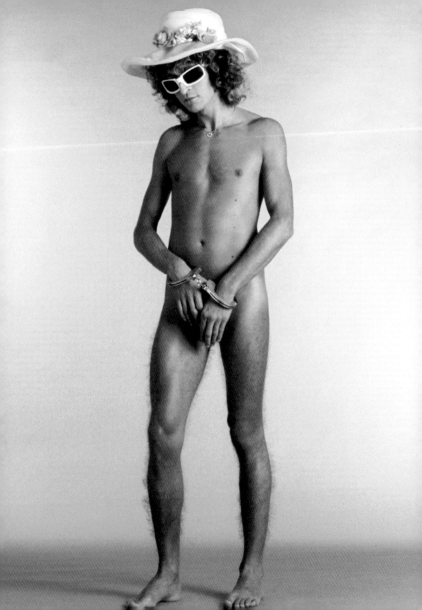

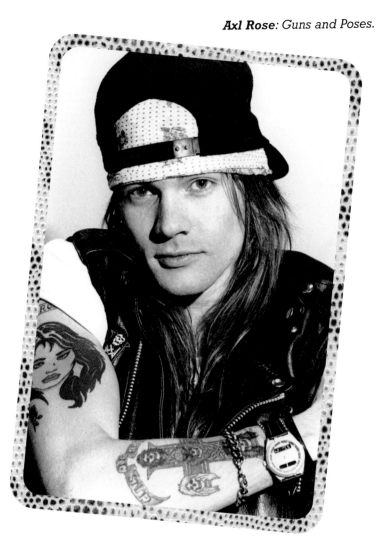

◀ ***Michel Polnareff*** *started to think his wedding outfit was misjudged.*

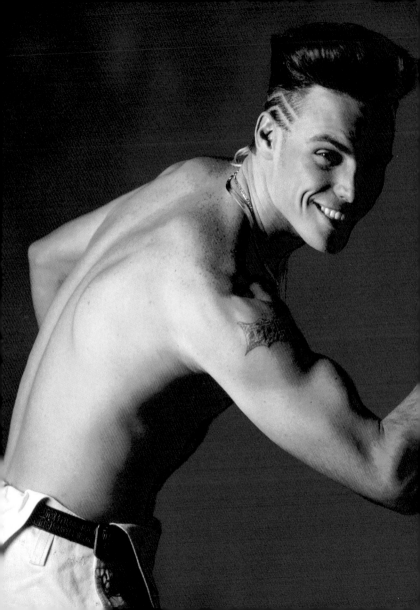

Vanilla Ice: everybody's favorite flavor.

*We go goo-goo over **Limahl**.*

Miles O'Keeffe: *You Tarzan,* ▶
we game for anything...

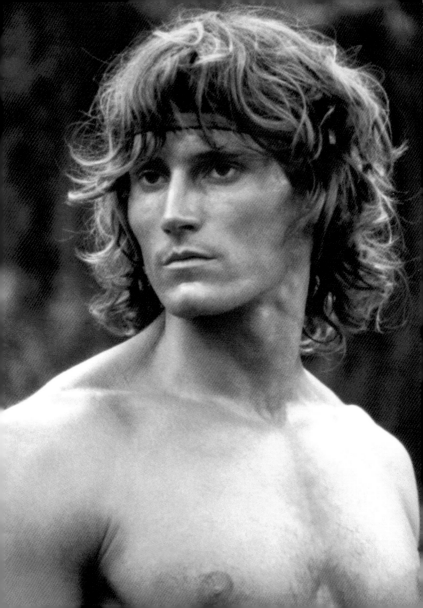

Bruce Springsteen: *born with a passion for line-dancing fashion.*

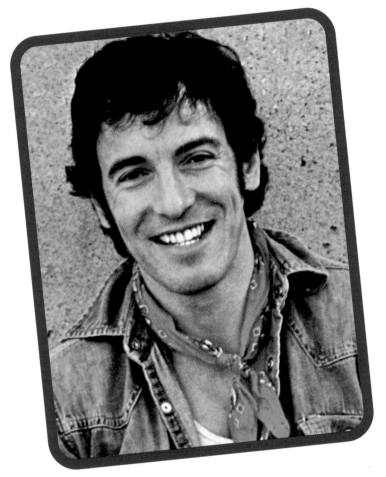

Judd *"Stud"* ▶
Nelson.

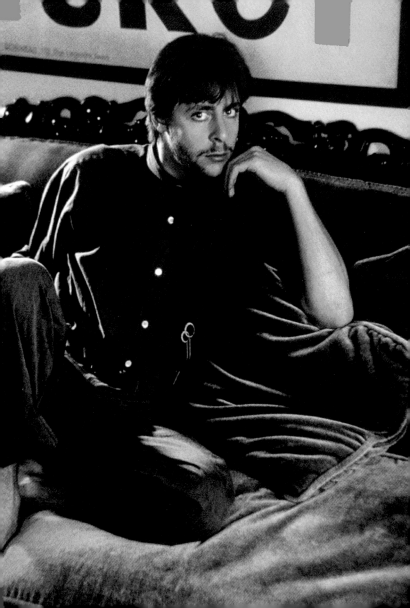

*George: **Best** before 1980.*

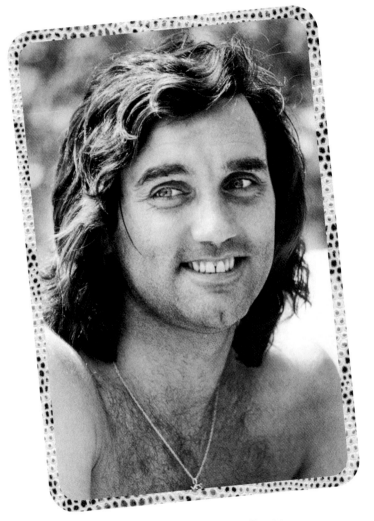

***Paul Newman** drives ▶
us wild in the West.*

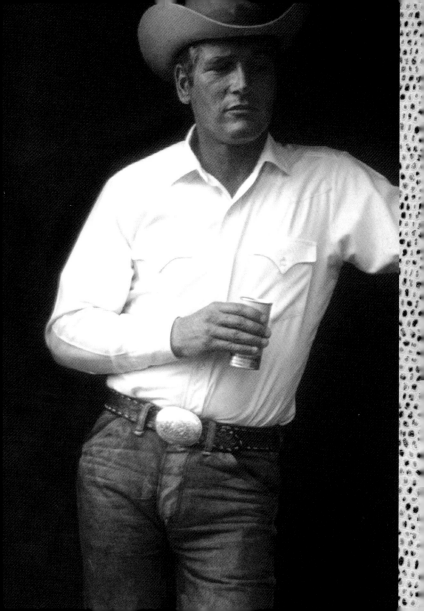

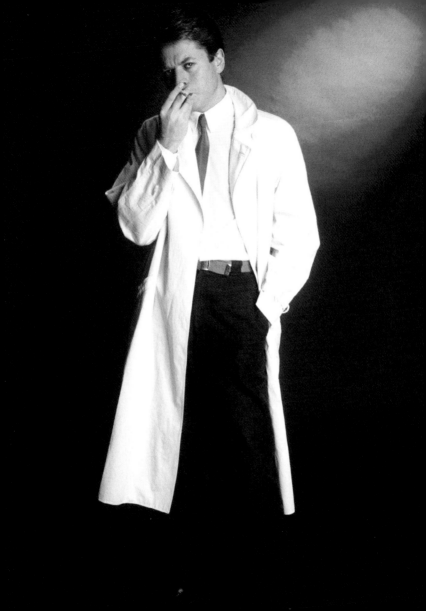

Oliver Tobias: The Stud. *Need we say more?*

◀ *Robert Palmer:* *smell my fingers.*

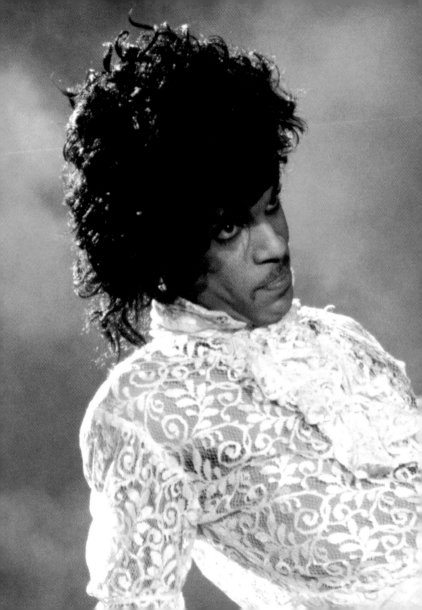

__Prince:__ sex symbol.

Michael J. Foxy

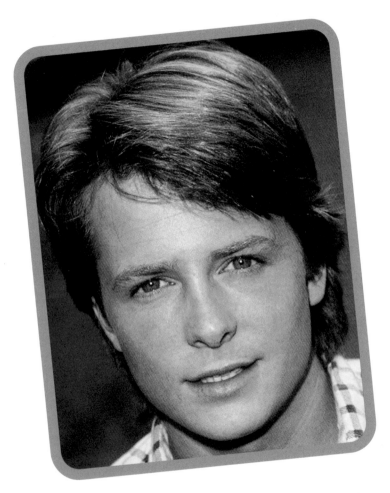

Richard gets ▶
his **Gere** off.

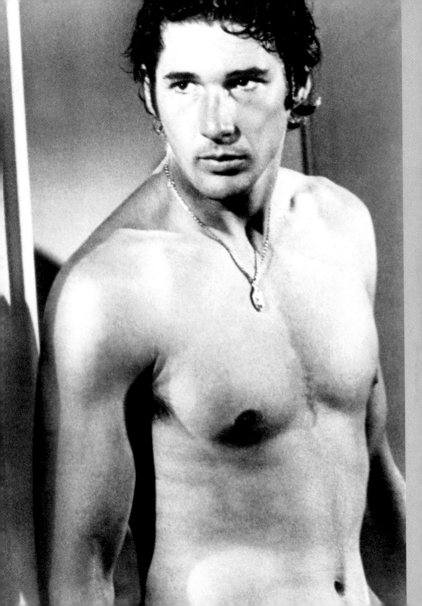

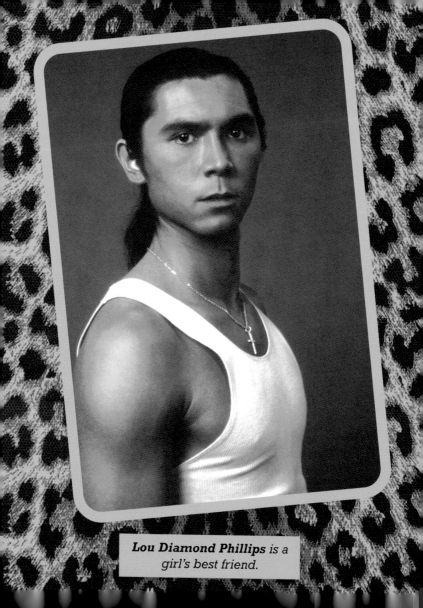

Lou Diamond Phillips is a
girl's best friend.

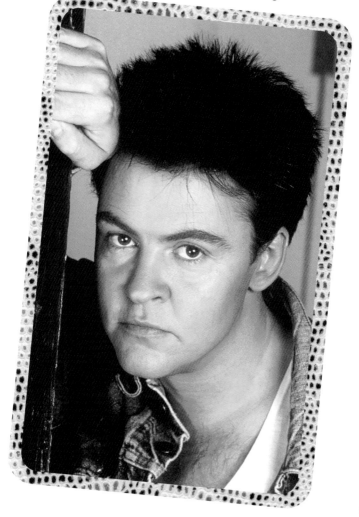

Paul Young looks calm,
despite trapping his
fingers in the door.

Morten Harket:
worth taking on.

Tim Robbins: ▶
oven ready.

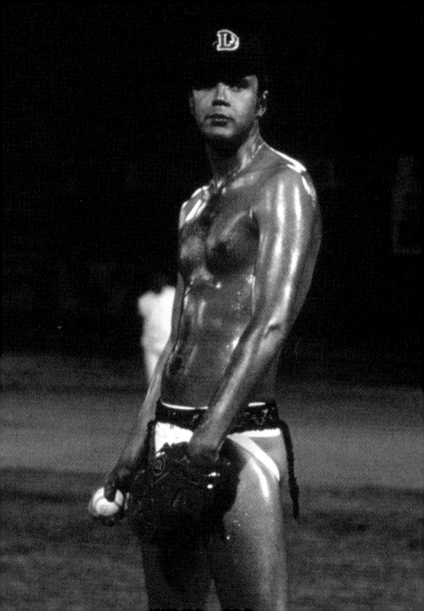

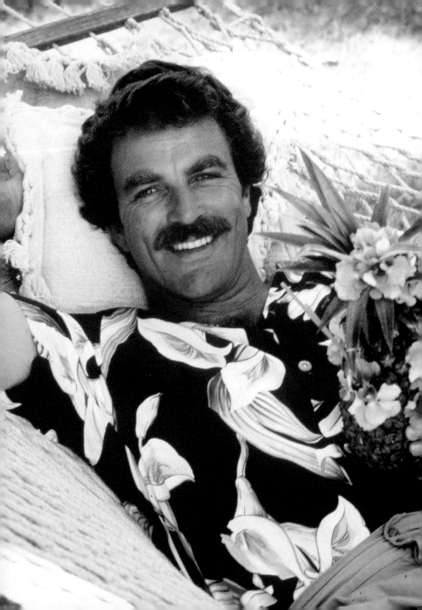

Michael Caine's not after
an Italian Job *with come-on
eyes like that . . .*

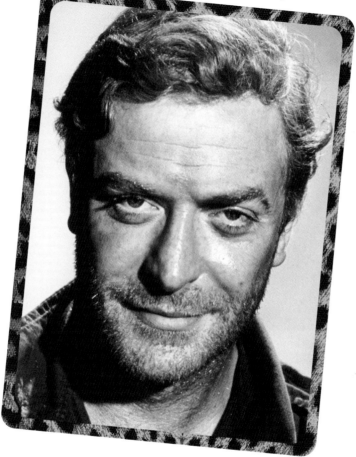

◀ *Tom Selleck: Anyone fancy
a lick of this* Magnum?

67

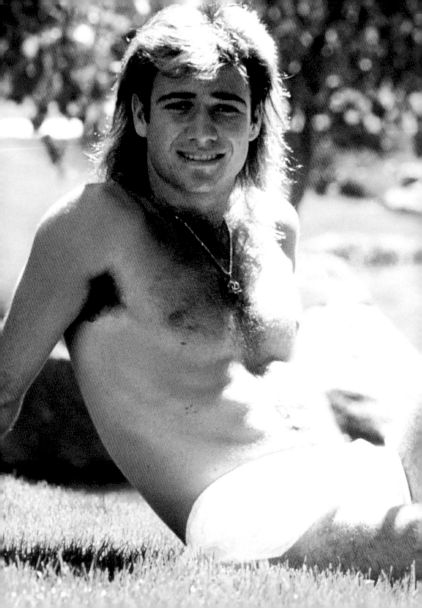

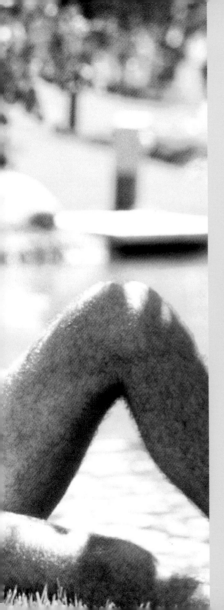

Andre Agassi: *game,
set, and wax?*

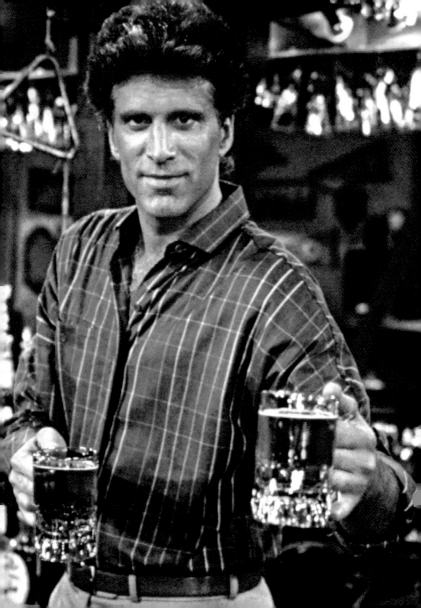

Whitesnake's **David Coverdale**: body of an athlete, hair of a dog.

Cheers, **Ted Danson**!

71

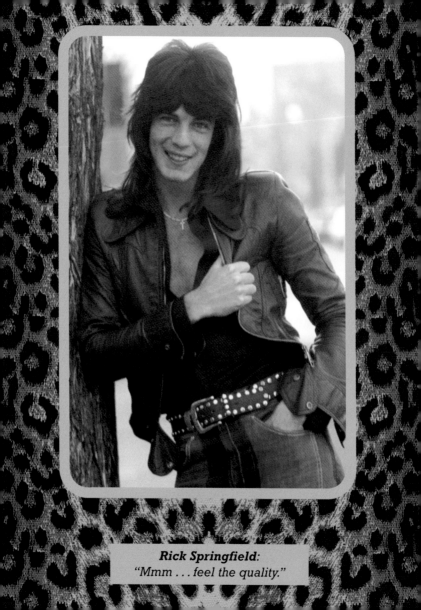

Rick Springfield:
"Mmm . . . feel the quality."

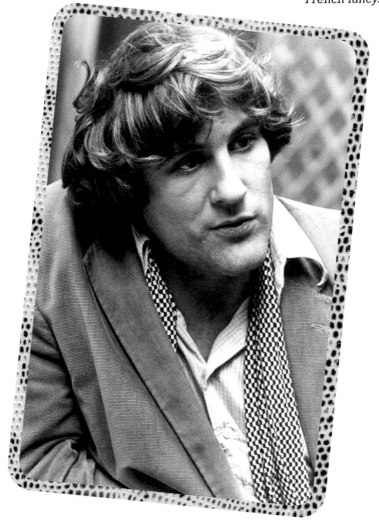

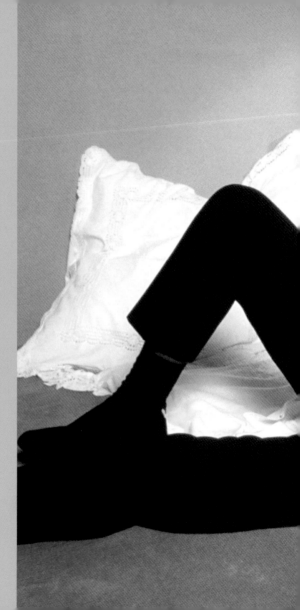

Simon Le Bon:
you can leave
your socks on.

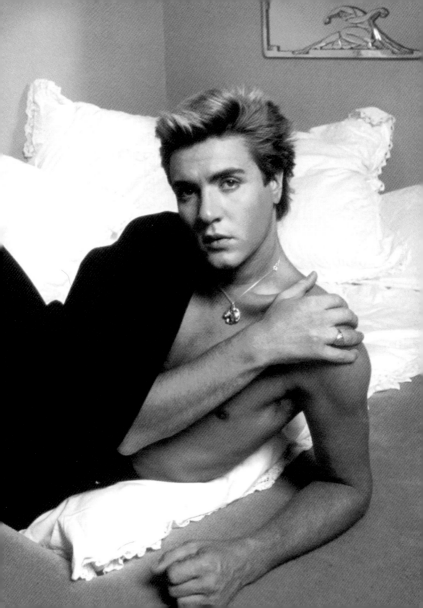

Marc Bolan: *look at the tits on that!*

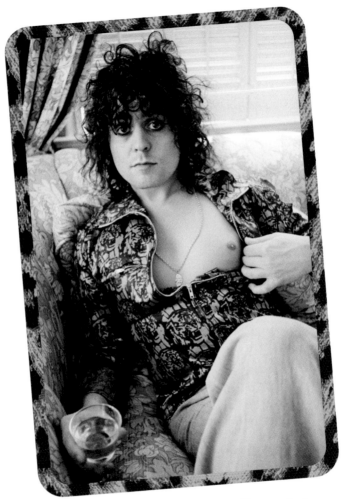

Can we help you with ▶
your handcuffs, Officer
(Steve) Guttenberg?

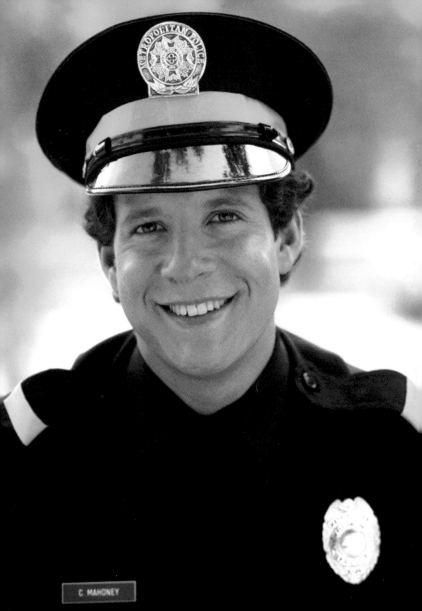

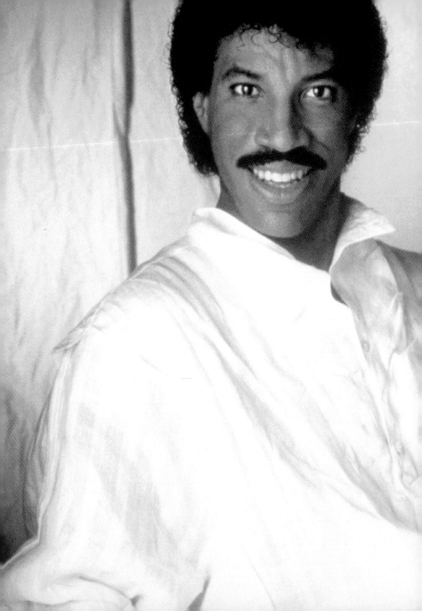

Lionel Richie: once, twice, three times a ladies' man.

*Don't tempt Bouncer with your sausage, **Craig McLachlan**.*

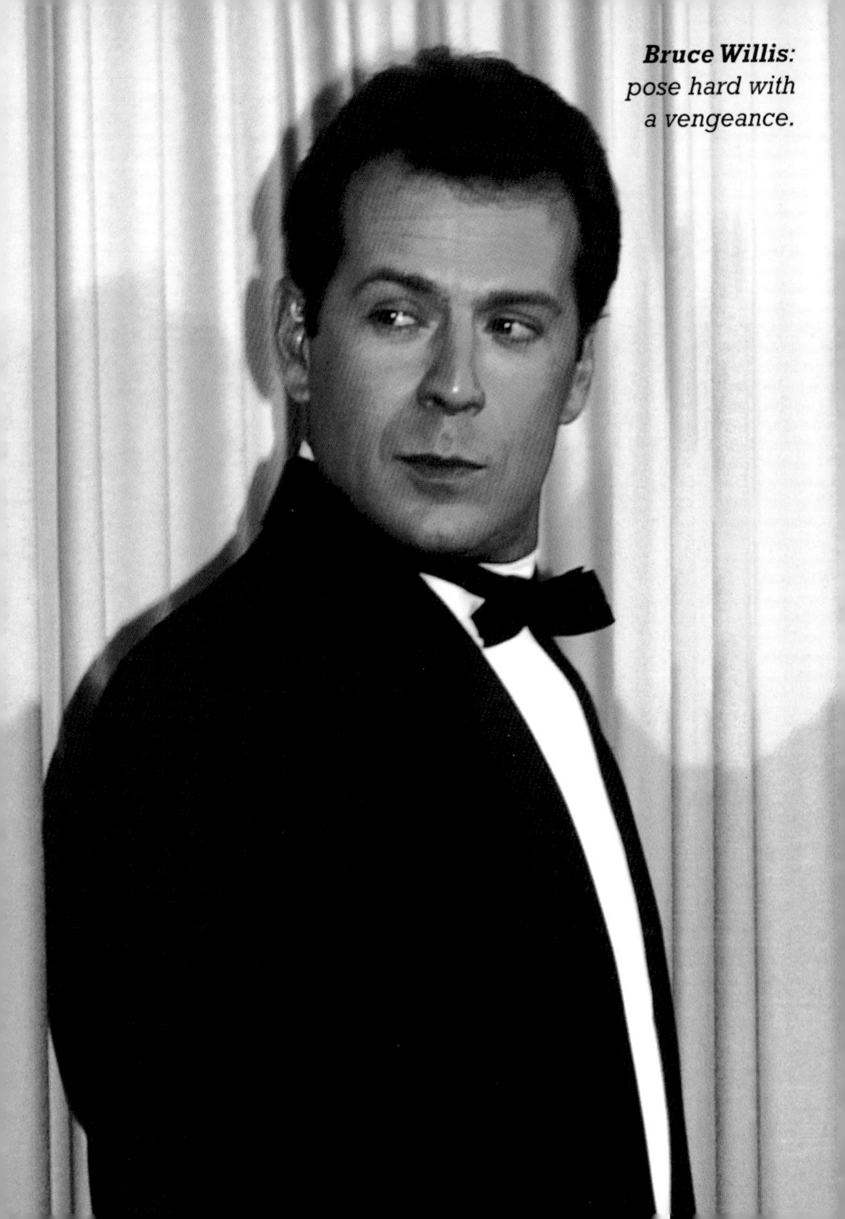

Bruce Willis: *pose hard with a vengeance.*

Barry White: *built for comfort, not for speed.*

*Is that a microphone in your ▶ pants, **Mick Jagger**, or are you just pleased to see us?*

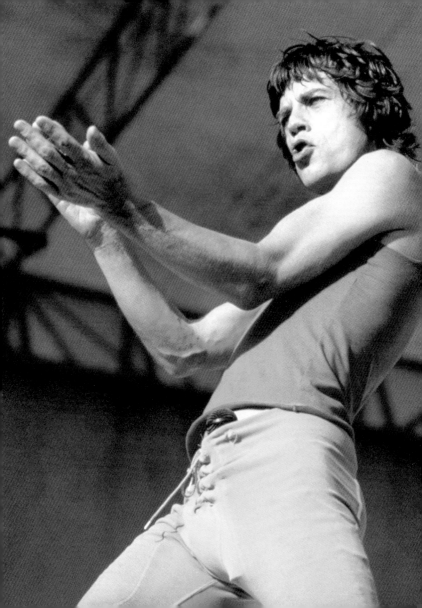

Julio Iglesias: *all teeth and torso.*

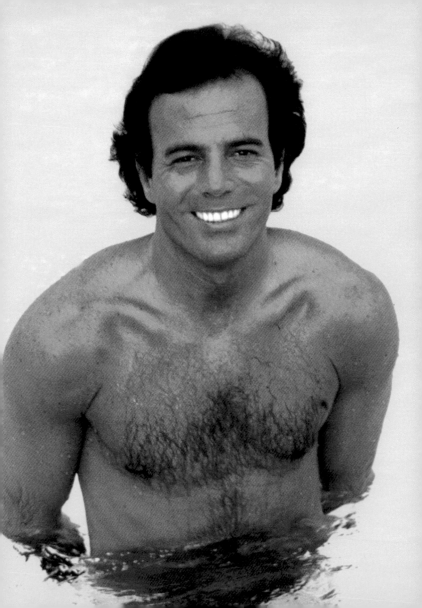

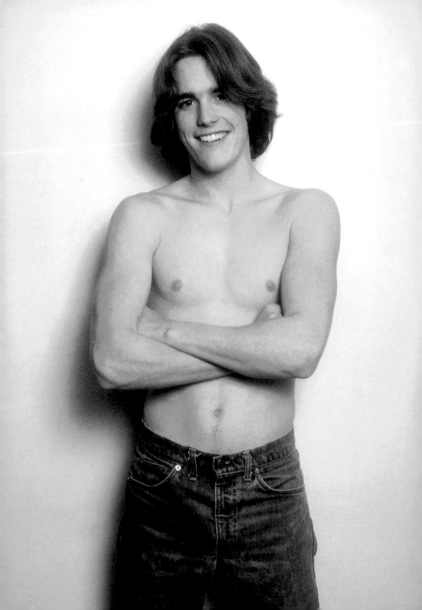

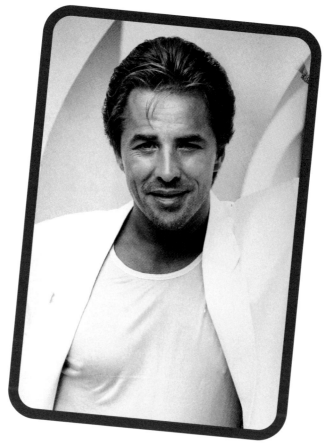

◀ **Matt Dillon**:
simply to die for.

Van Halen's
David Lee Roth:
*small trousers,
big hair.*

*It wasn't just the length of **Tom Hanks**'s stem that impressed the ladies.*

Tony Blackburn *shows off his Lego hair.*

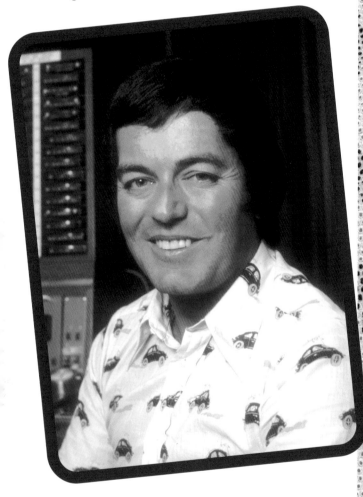

We love a man in ▶ uniform, **Sean Penn**.

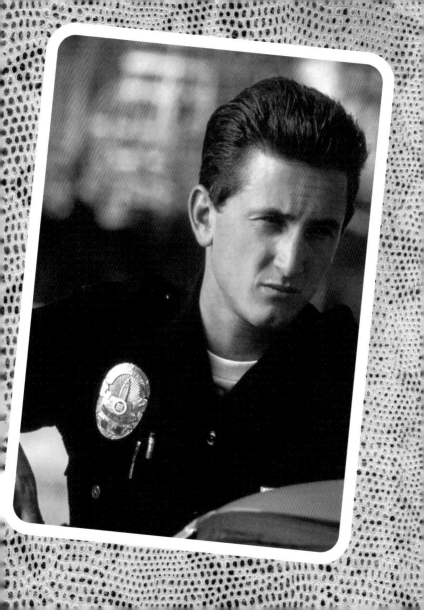

Bryan Ferry: suave, sophisticated . . . and somewhat sinister.

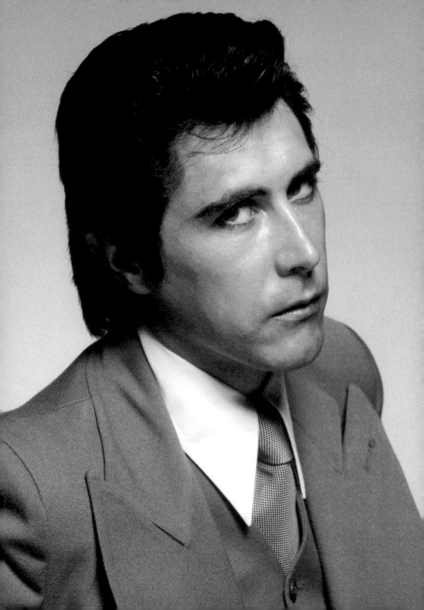

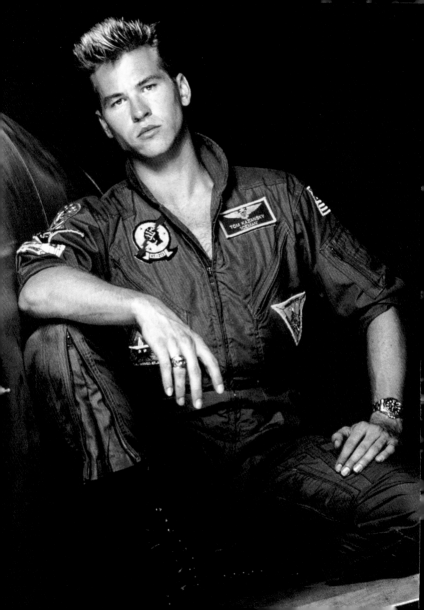

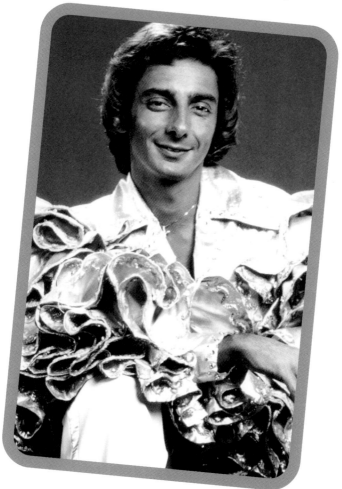

*That outfit should be copacabanned, **Barry Manilow**.*

◀ **Val Kilmer:**
the Iceman cometh ...

95

Jason Donovan:
*the original boy
next door.*

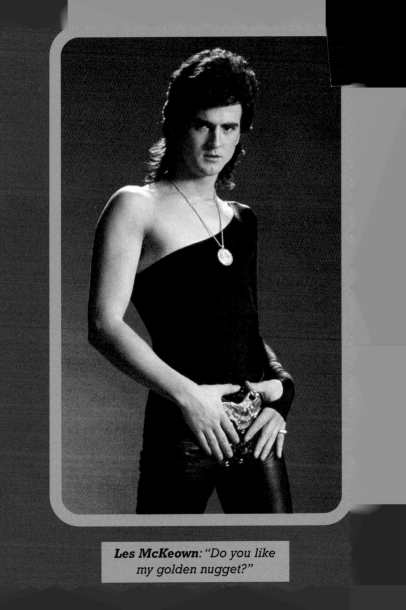

Les McKeown: "Do you like my golden nugget?"

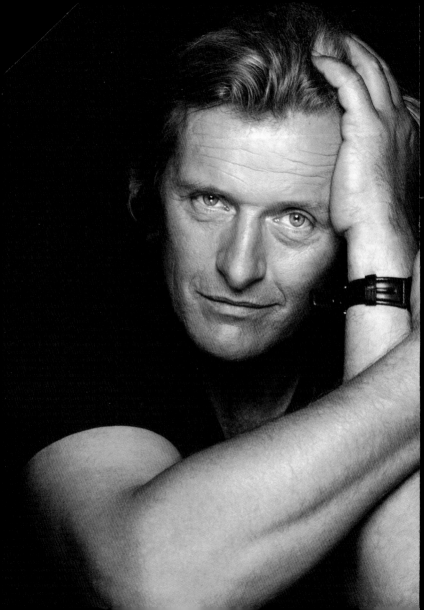

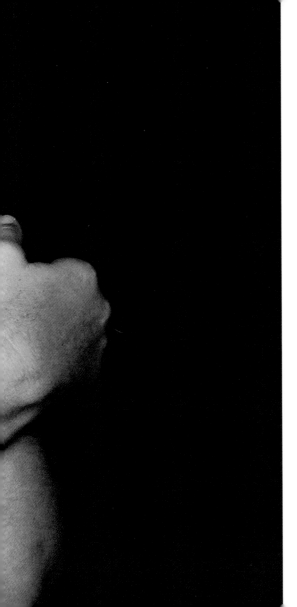

Rutger Hauer:
good things come
to those who wait.

Lee Majors: *six-million-dollar six-pack.*

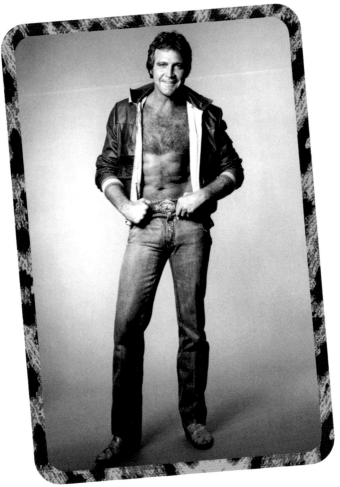

Errol Brown *from* ▶
Hot Chocolate:
knight in white satin.

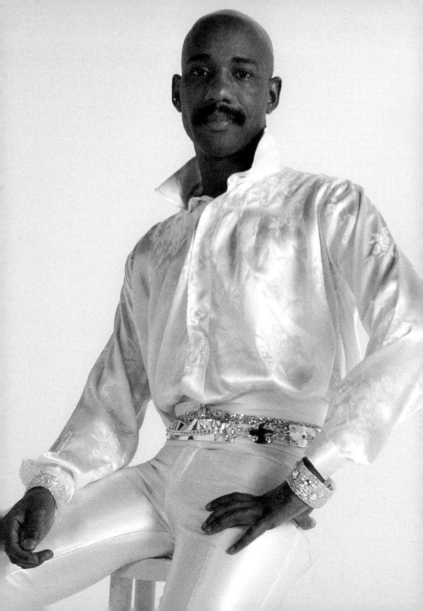

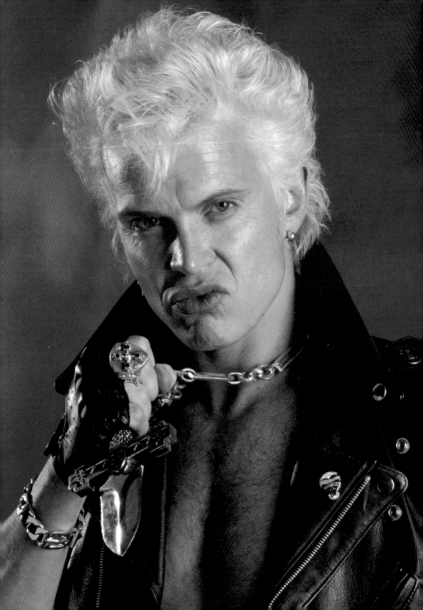

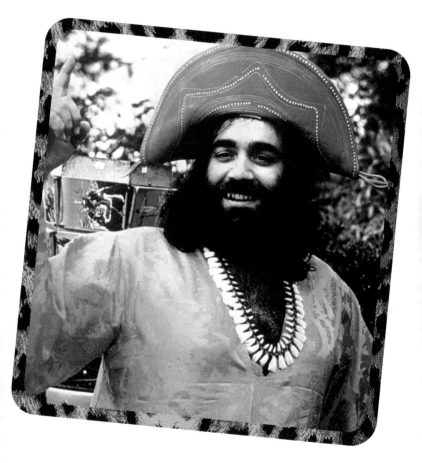

◀ **Billy Idol**
yanks his chain.

103

Bros: *take two into the shower.*

Charlie Sheen: *a Hot Shot*
by anyone's standards.

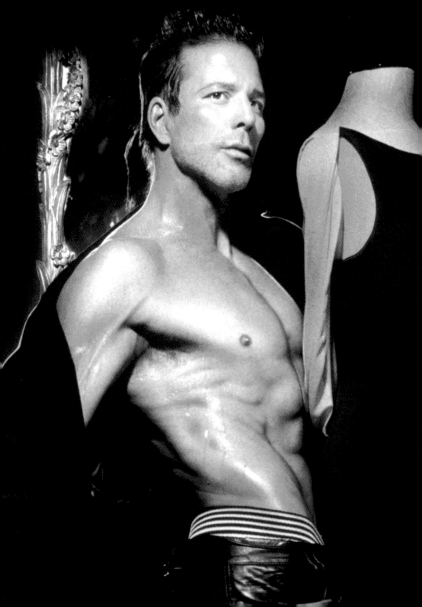

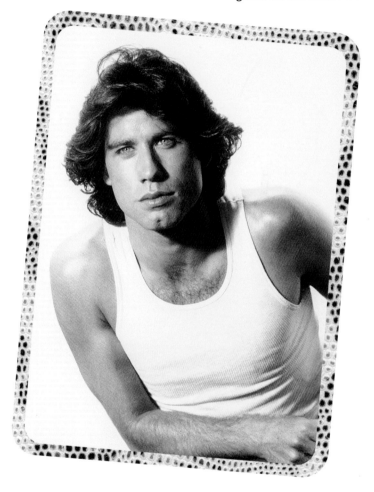

◀ *Oh **Mickey (Rourke)**, you're so fine . . .*

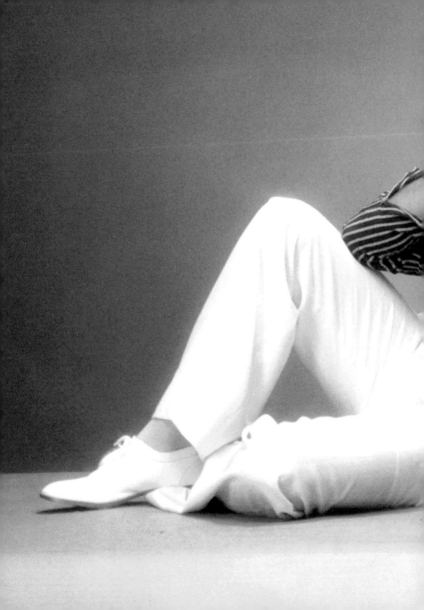

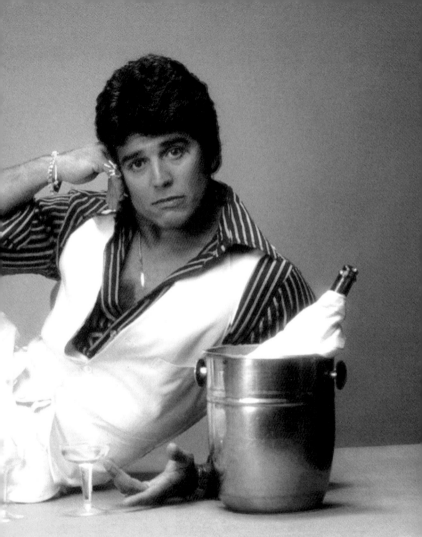

Erik Estrada *wonders if his seduction technique is looking a little obvious.*

Sean Connery: *double "oh" heaven.*

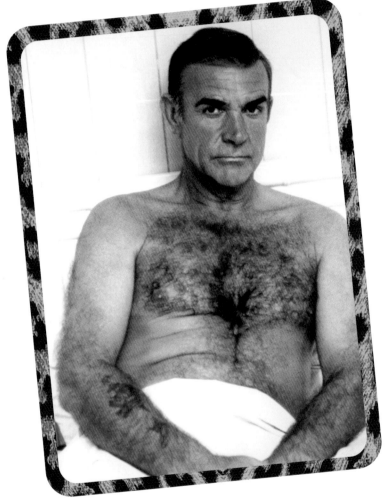

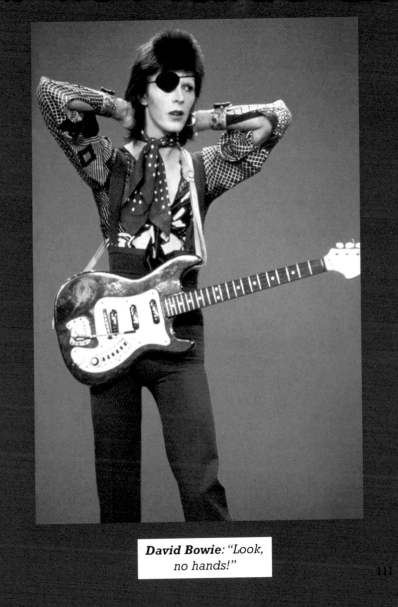

David Bowie: *"Look, no hands!"*

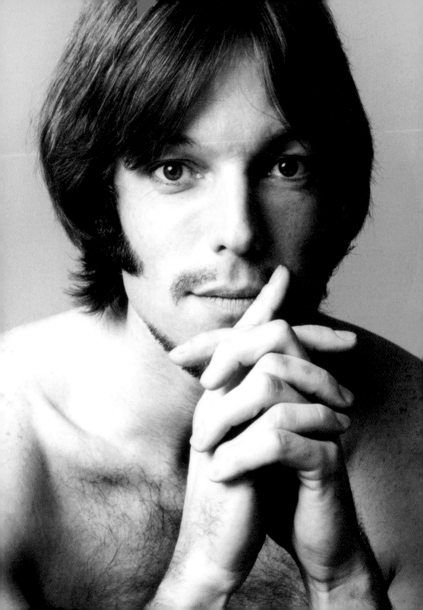

John James: we'd like to
ride this cowboy.

◀ *Richard Chamberlain:*
Dr. Killer Stare.

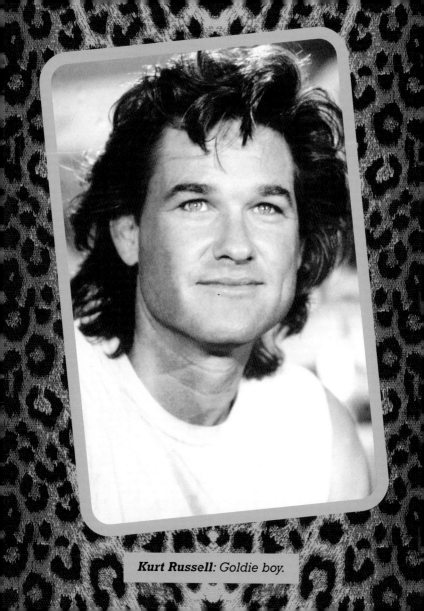

Kurt Russell: *Goldie boy.*

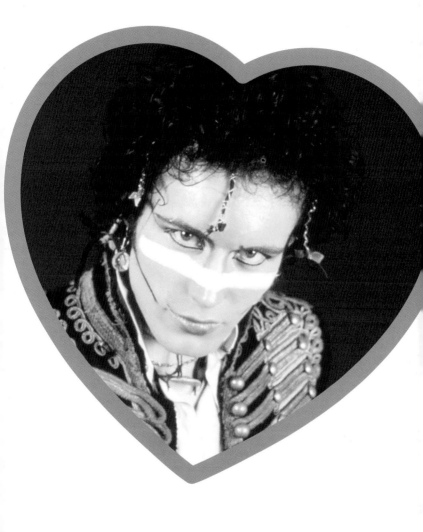

Adam Ant: Prince Charming.

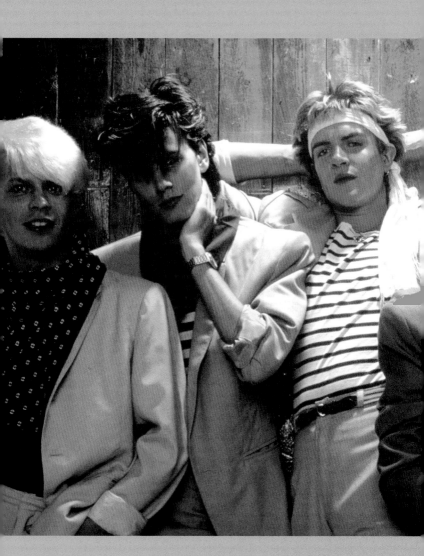

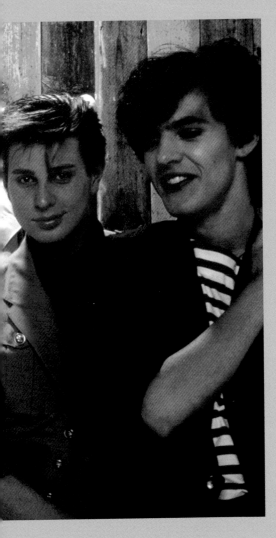

Duran Duran: *these wild boys are so good they named them twice.*

117

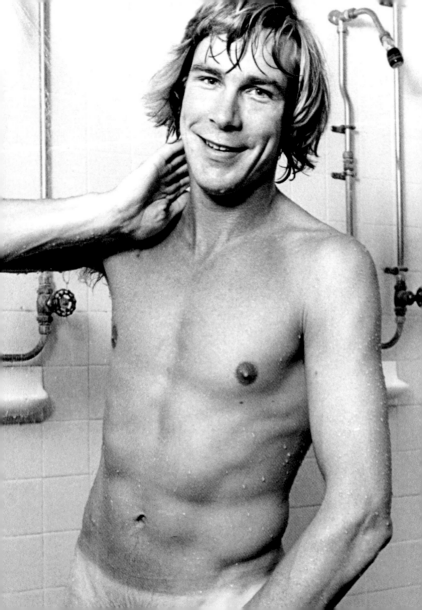

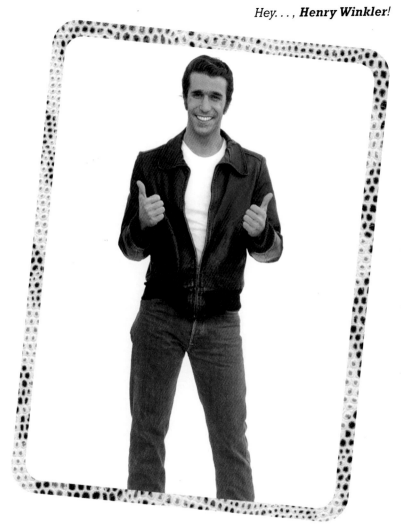

◀ **James Hunt** *just misses out on showing us his pole position.*

George Clooney: *he's a lumberjack and he's (more than) OK.*

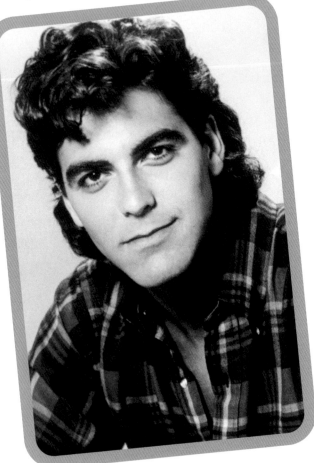

Wham!: *The teeth are* ▶ *bright, the skin is orange.*

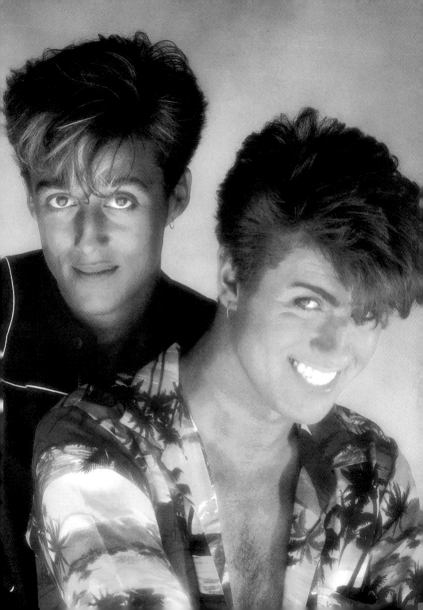

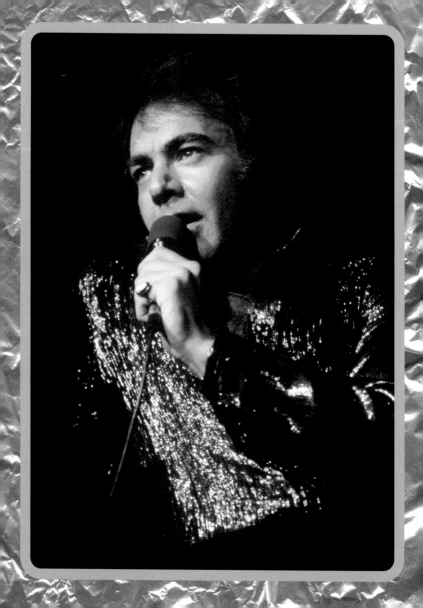

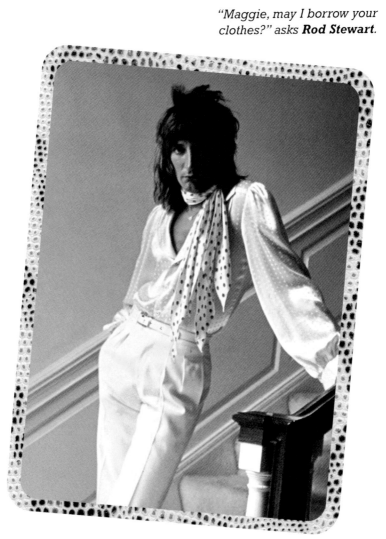

◀ **Neil Diamond** *wishes he'd used Head & Shoulders.*

Roger Moore—*with a name like that, he was guaranteed a place in the God's Gift Hall of Fame.*

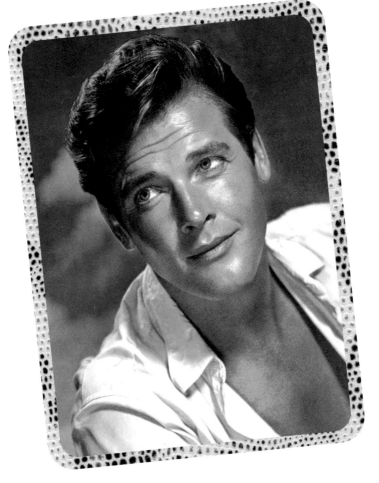

Matthew Broderick: ▶
the cable-knit guy.

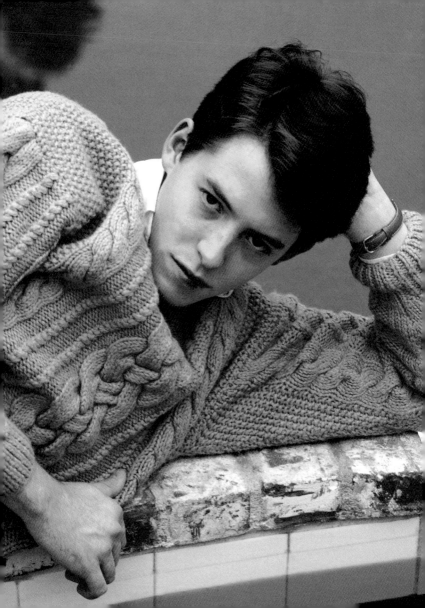

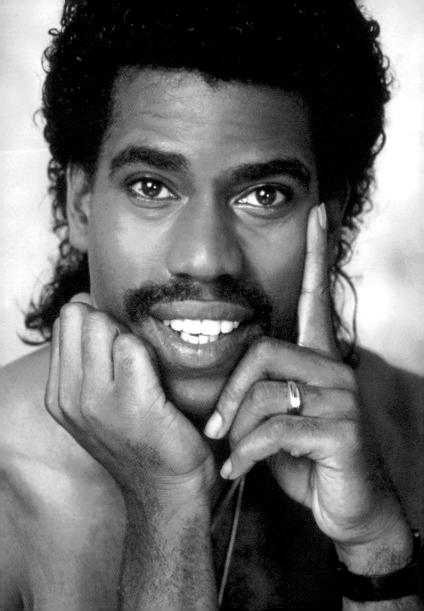

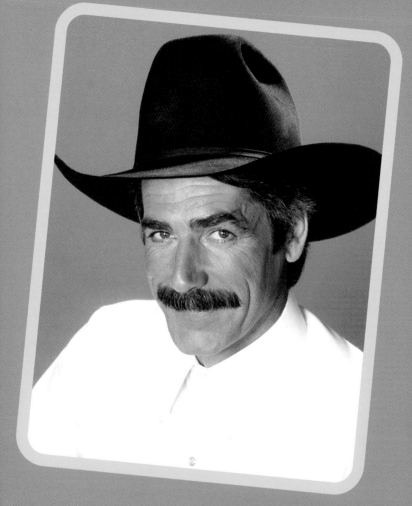

◀ **Kurtis Blow** rates his hair-style out of ten.

Does Daisy know you've been using her hair products, **John Schneider**?

Patrick Duffy: Ewing—y'would. ▶

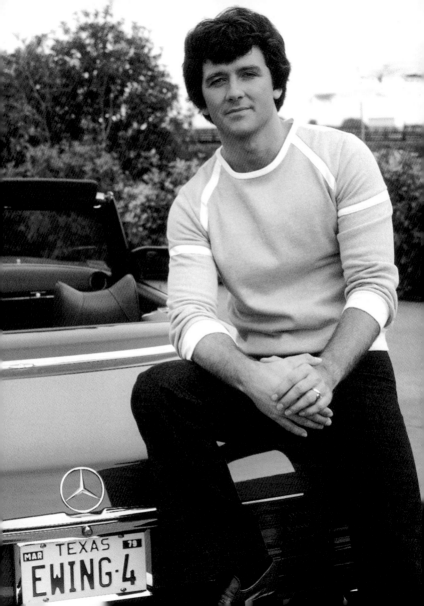

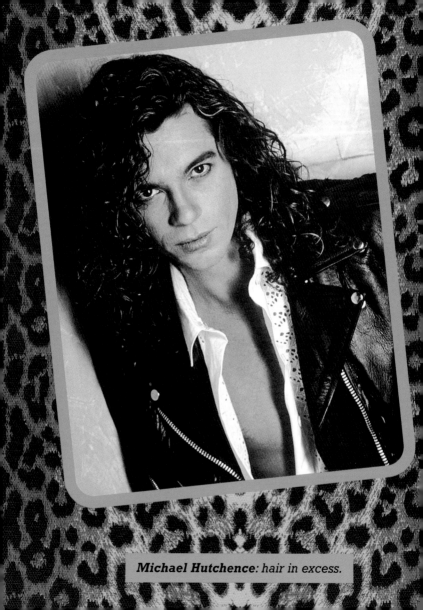

Michael Hutchence: *hair in excess.*

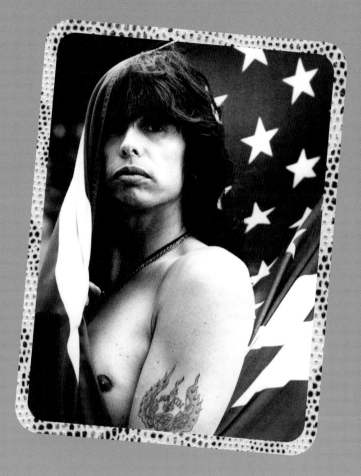

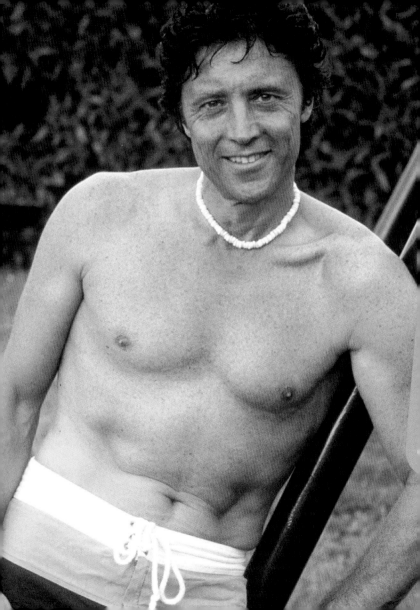

Brad Pitt: Troy *boy.*

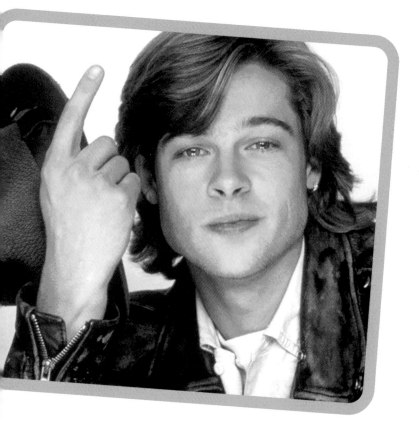

◀ **Sacha Distel:** voulez-vous
coucher avec moi, ce soir?

Harrison Ford doesn't
have to go solo.

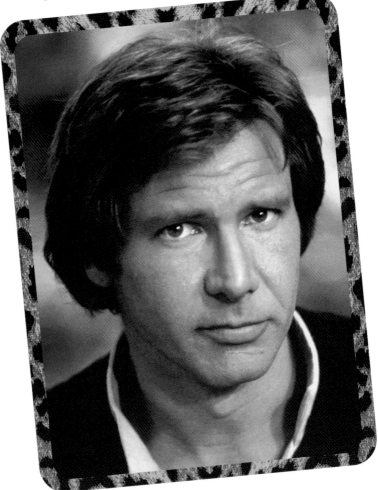

We'd help **Kris Kristofferson** ▶
make it through the night any day.

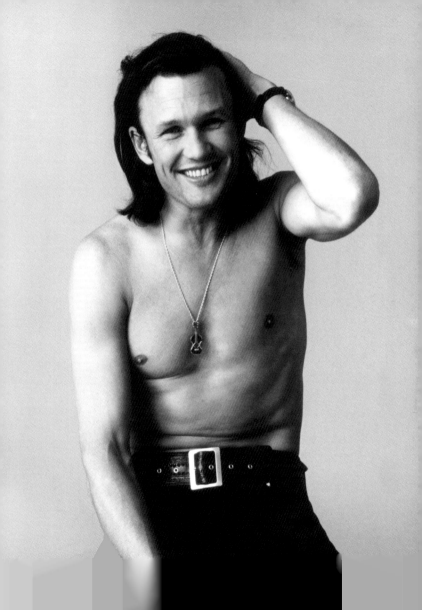

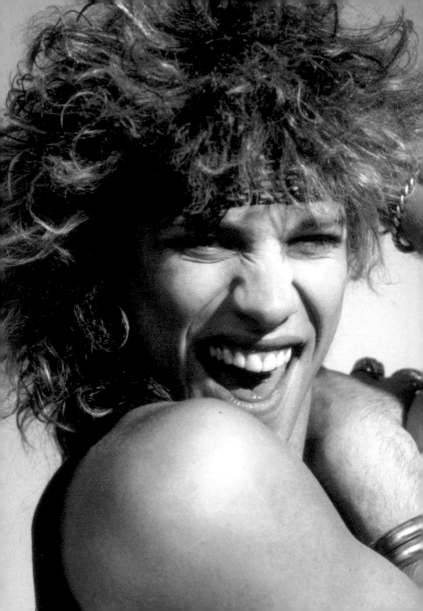

Pierce Brosnan *knows how to*
Remington Steele *our hearts.*

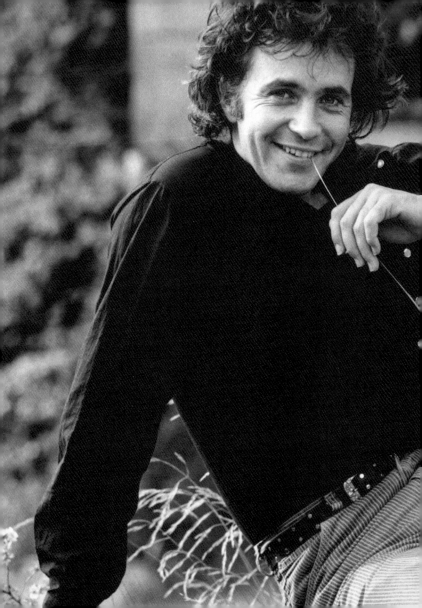

David: the man who puts the "sex" into "**Essex**."

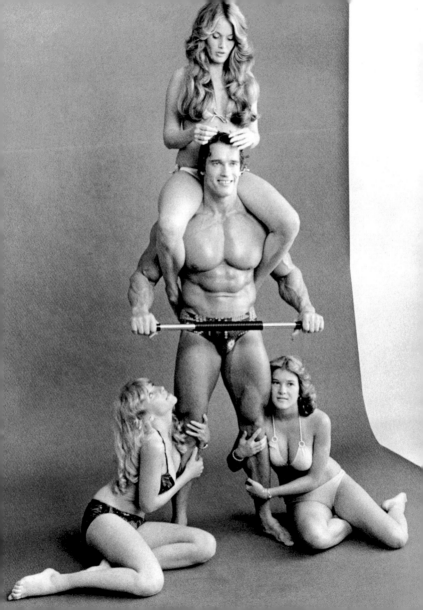

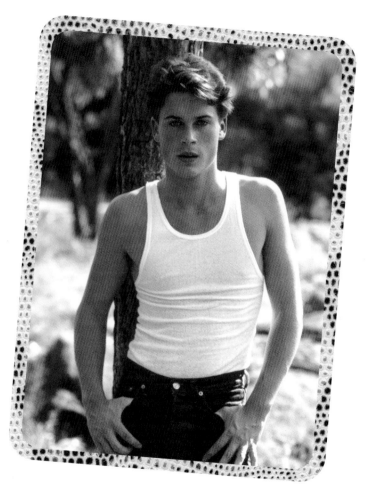

◀ **Arnold Schwarzenegger**: *the Governator*
demonstrates his impeccable taste.

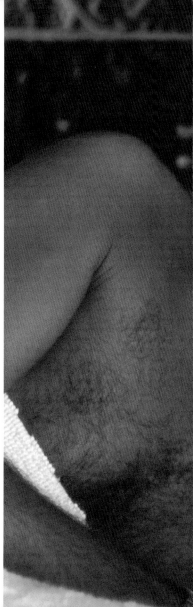

Tom Jones:
boyo, oh boyo!

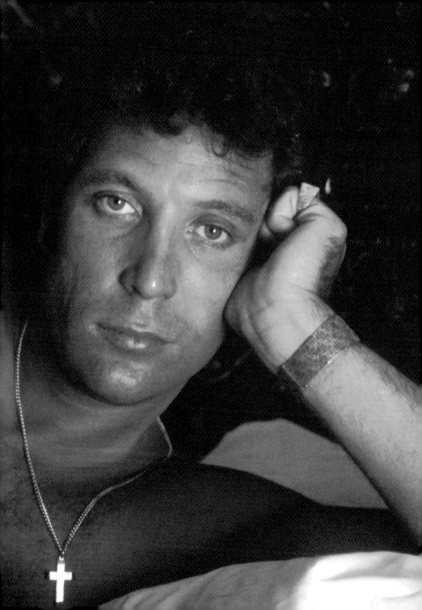

Picture Credits

p. 53 Sipa Press/Rex Features

p. 54 © Bettman/Corbis

p. 55 Rex Features

p. 56 Rex Features

p. 57 Richard Young/Rex Features

p. 58–9 © Neal Preston/Corbis

p. 60 Kip Rano/Rex Features

p. 61 SNAP/Rex Features

p. 62 SNAP/Rex Features

p. 63 Rex Features

p. 64 Ilpo Musto/Rex Features

p. 65 SNAP/Rex Features

p. 66 CBS–TV/The Kobal Collection

p. 67 SNAP/Rex Features

p. 68–9 Peter Stone/Rex Features

p. 70 Everett Collection/Rex
Features

p. 71 Dave Hogan/Hulton Archive/
Getty Images

p. 72 © Henry Diltz/Corbis

p. 73 Araldo di Crollalanza/Rex
Features

p. 74–5 Andy Rosen/Rex Features

p. 76 © Neal Preston/Corbis

p. 77 SNAP/Rex Features

p. 78–9 Araldo di Crollalanza/Rex
Features

p. 80 Brendan Beirne/Rex Features

p. 81 © Walter McBride/Retna Ltd

p. 82 © Patricia Steur/Sunshine/
Retna

p. 83 © Lynn Goldsmith/Corbis

p. 84–5 Santi Visalli/Getty Images

p. 86 Robin Platzer/Time Life
Pictures/Getty Images

p. 87 Allstar

p. 88 © Lynn Goldsmith/Corbis

p. 89 Deborah Feingold/Getty
Images

p. 90 © BBC Photo Library/Redferns

p. 91 Orion/The Kobal Collection

p. 92–3 Terry O'Neill / Hulton
Archive/Getty Images

p. 94 Paramount/The Kobal
Collection

p. 95 Pictorial Press

p. 96 Adrian Boot/RetnaUK

p. 97 © Fin Costello/Redferns

p. 98–9 Terry O'Neill/Getty Images

p. 100 ABC–TV: The Kobal
Collection

p. 101 © Fin Costello/Redferns

p. 102 © Neal Preston/Corbis

p. 103 © GAB Archives/Redferns

p. 104 © Neil Mathews/RetnaUK/
Retna Ltd, USA

p. 105 © Sandra Johnson/RetnaUK

p. 106 © Kal Yee/Retna Ltd

Acknowledgments

A GREAT MANY people have been involved in the making of this book. The editors would like to thank the whole team at Michael O'Mara Books, especially Jane Carson, for the original ideas and brainstorming sessions. Thanks also to Miranda Sheath and Claire Banyard for their contribution to the *God's Gift* wish list; and to Lindsay Davies, Matt Foss, Kate Gribble, Louise Hall, Tanveer Minhas, Duncan Moore, Hannah Robinson, Ana Sampson, Ruth Shippobotham, and Tim Stapleton for the captions. Lucie Cave provided the fabulous foreword, while Envy Design have excelled with the design of both the cover and insides.

Finally, sincere thanks to Judith Palmer, picture researcher extraordinaire, who had the enviable task of spending hours tracking down the sexiest, funniest, hunkiest pictures of the studs, stallions, and dreamboats who fill these pages. It was a tough job, but someone had to do it.

Designed by www.envydesign.co.uk

Library of Congress Cataloging-in-Publication Data

God's gift : over 100 studs, stallions, and dreamboats from the 70s
and 80s / foreword by Lucie Cave.
    p. cm.
  ISBN 13: 978-0-8109-9451-5
  ISBN 10: 0-8109-9451-8
  1. Male actors—United States—Portraits. 2. Male singers—United
States—Portraits.

  PN2285G63 2007
  791.4302'80810973—dc22
                                    2007004730

First published in 2006 by Michael O'Mara Books Limited, 9 Lion
Yard, Tremadoc Road, London SW4 7NQ

Printed and bound in Singapore
10 9 8 7 6 5 4 3 2 1

HNA ▮▮▮▮▮
harry n. abrams, inc.
a subsidiary of La Martinière Groupe

115 West 18th Street
New York, NY 10011
www.hnabooks.com